TORNA

THE STORY BEHIND THESE
TWISTING, TURNING, SPINNING,
AND SPIRALING STORMS

DO!

by JUDITH BLOOM FRADIN & DENNIS BRINDELL FRADIN

NATIONAL GEOGRAPHIC
WASHINGTON, D.C.

CONTENTS

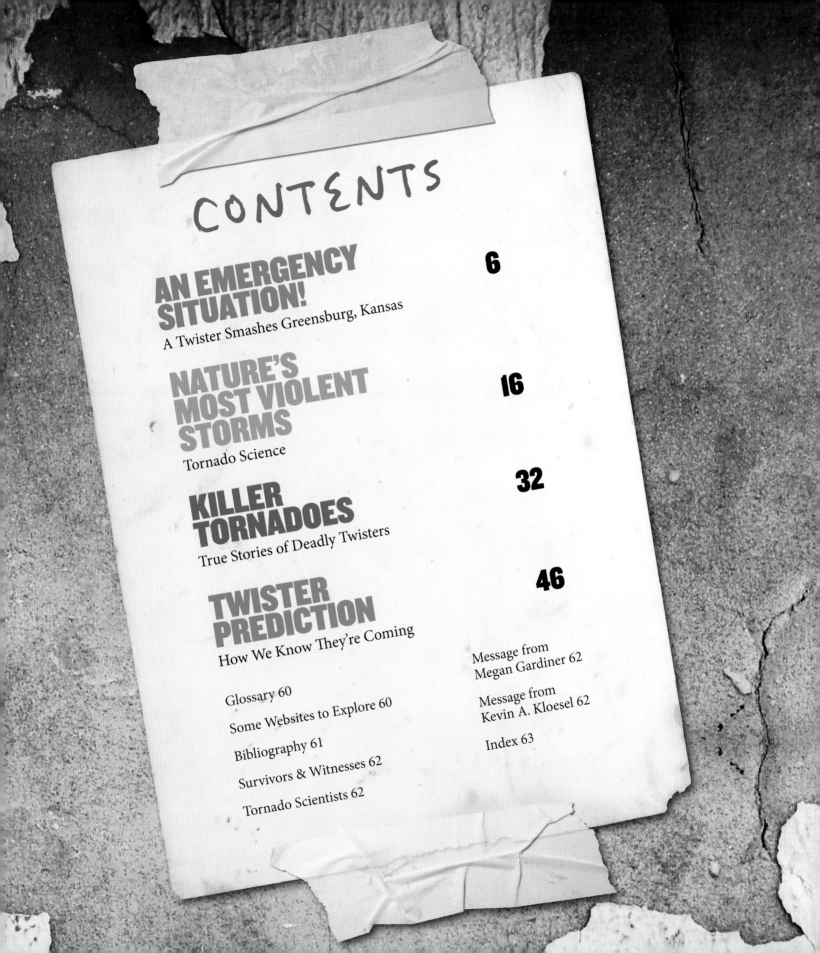

AN EMERGENCY SITUATION!

A Twister Smashes Greensburg, Kansas

A 1.7-mile-wide (2.7 km) monstrous twister advances on Greensburg, Kansas—most of which was destroyed minutes later.

"IT'S NOTHING LIKE THE PICTURES AND TV. IN REAL LIFE IT'S 100 TIMES WORSE BECAUSE YOU SEE EVERYTHING JUST SHREDDED AND RIPPED INTO PIECES."

Megan Gardiner,
-tornado survivor

AT 9:00 P.M. ON MAY 4, 2007, A TORNADO FORMED IN KANSAS and roared toward Greensburg, a city of 1,600 people. This monstrous twister was 1.7 miles (2.7 km) wide—15 times larger than an average tornado. Frequent lightning illuminated the approaching twister, enabling several storm chasers and police to spot it and notify authorities.

The tornado also lit up radar screens at the National Weather Service office in Dodge City, Kansas, 40 miles (64 km) northwest of Greensburg. At 9:19 P.M. meteorologist Mike Umscheid issued the following tornado warning to Greensburg officials as well as to local TV and radio stations:

A LARGE AND EXTREMELY DANGEROUS TORNADO 14 MILES SOUTH OF GREENSBURG. . .TAKE COVER IN A BASEMENT OR OTHER UNDERGROUND SHELTER AND GET UNDER SOMETHING STURDY.

By 9:25 P.M., officials in Greensburg had activated the city's tornado sirens. The sirens were blaring when 17-year-old Megan Gardiner left her restaurant job and sped home in her car. "When I busted through the front door, my dad was up there with a flashlight waiting for me," Megan later recalled. "He said, 'Go downstairs!'" Before joining her family and a few neighbors in their basement, Megan retrieved some valuables from her bedroom. "That's the last time I ever saw my room."

At 9:41 P.M. Umscheid issued a Tornado Emergency Bulletin—a warning released only when a large, long-lasting tornado is about to strike a specific locale:

A VIOLENT TORNADO IS ON A DIRECT PATH FOR PORTIONS OF GREENSBURG....THIS IS AN EMERGENCY SITUATION FOR GREENSBURG!!!

The humongous twister smashed into Greensburg four minutes later. No one who survived it will ever forget the moment the 200-mile-per-hour (322 km/h) winds struck. "It sounded like a jet engine going right over us, about to take off," Megan Gardiner remembers. "The windows exploded into millions of pieces. Just hearing the house rip into shreds was horrible."

It took the storm a few minutes to pass through town. Once it was gone, Megan and her family and friends crawled out from beneath the boards and other debris that had fallen upon them. When they looked up, they saw sky. The floors, ceiling, and roof of the Gardiner house had been ripped away. Miraculously, nobody in their basement was seriously injured.

"I felt our house lifting away—I felt the suction, the pulling," recalls Janice Haney, a Greensburg resident who survived the devastation with her husband, John, in their basement. "I thought we were going to be lifted away. It took about two or three minutes for the tornado to go over. After it passed, our house was gone and we had no stairs left to climb up out of our basement."

SURVIVORS later explained that their EARS HURT when the Greensburg tornado came through.

"My ears popped and I thought my head was going to explode."

RECALLS JANICE HANEY
Greensburg tornado survivor

People's ears hurt during a tornado because a twister has lower air pressure than the air around it. Because of the tornado's lower pressure, the pressure inside the ears becomes greater than the pressure outside the body. This sucks the eardrums outward, which is painful.

BEFORE

11:23

AFTER

Megan Gardiner's brother Matt and their friend Mike Ray stare dumbfounded at the devastation of their neighborhood. The fragments of red fabric are pieces of Megan and Matt's parents' bedroom rug. The inset picture shows the Gardiner house before the Greensburg tornado struck.

9

The devastating tornado tossed this blue minivan into what used to be a Greensburg motel.

Megan Gardiner's family lived across the street from the Greensburg High School. This is how the school's new gymnasium looked after the tornado.

Many people were trapped beneath the debris of their homes. "The back part of my house fell into the basement and heavy boards and lumber pinned me down," says Sheri Taylor. "I couldn't move except for one hand, and I couldn't even turn my head. Around midnight a rescue crew came to my house and heard where my voice was coming from. They used a chain saw to cut away boards to get to me, then took hold of my arms and pulled me straight up out of there. I had been pinned for two hours."

Although the electricity had been knocked out, flashes of lightning revealed scenes of incredible destruction. "No trees, no houses, nothing," recalls Janice Haney. Adds Dea Corns: "When I saw the town by daylight I just cried. I got lost two blocks from my house on the street I had lived on for fourteen years because all the landmarks were gone."

Nearly 1,000 homes and businesses—95 percent of the buildings in Greensburg—were destroyed. Yet despite the 200-mile-per-hour (322 km/h) winds, falling trees, flying debris, and flattened homes, something remarkable occurred. A death toll in the hundreds might have been expected, but thanks to National Weather Service warnings and to citizens who heeded them, the Greensburg tornado claimed only 11 lives.

SURVIVORS say they will never forget the MUSTY, MOLDY SMELL of their town after the Greensburg tornado.

"I salvaged a few things from my house and stored them in my aunt and uncle's garage. But later when I went over to wash the things off I got a whiff of that smell and it made me flash back to the tornado. I had to get out of there."

SHERI TAYLOR
Greensburg tornado survivor

Twelve days after the 200 mph (322 km/h) tornadic winds ripped through Greensburg, Kansas, the center of town was still a scene of mass destruction.

1

Twisters are
born in
THUNDERSTORMS
and are often
accompanied by
HAIL.

2

Tornadoes
usually
**DON'T KILL
PEOPLE.**
Collapsing buildings
and flying debris
are the killers.

3

"TORNADO ALLEY"—
a broad band stretching down
the middle of the U.S.—has
MORE TORNADOES
than anywhere else
in the world.

6

Twisters are
most likely
to form between
the hours of
**3 P.M. AND
9 P.M.**

7

Tornadoes
have struck
**ALL 50
STATES.**

8

In appearance, tornadoes
have been compared to an
**ELEPHANT'S TRUNK,
THE LIBERTY BELL,
A MUSHROOM STEM,
A TREE TRUNK,
AND A ROPE.**

4

Most tornadoes
in the Northern
Hemisphere
ROTATE
COUNTER-CLOCKWISE.
Almost all tornadoes
in the Southern
Hemisphere
ROTATE
CLOCKWISE.

5

Tornado
winds are the
STRONGEST
IN THE
WORLD.

9

Outside the U.S.,
ARGENTINA AND
BANGLADESH
record the
MOST TORNADOES
ANNUALLY.

10

Tornadoes
come in
ALL COLORS
because they take
on the color of
materials they
pick up.

A "dust devil"—a whirlwind somewhat similar
to a tornado—struck the northeast African
nation of Djibouti in 2008. In Australia, such
whirlwinds are called "willy-willies."

NATURE'S MOST VIOLENT STORMS

Tornado Science

As his assistant drove backward to escape a tornado, photographer Jim Reed snapped this photo of a Kansas state trooper's car. Here you see the trooper's back-up lights as he avoided the oncoming twister.

WEIGHT
LIMIT
8
TONS

"TO ME, TORNADOES SOUND LIKE THE SPACE SHUTTLE OR A ROCKET TAKING OFF. THIS ROAR IS CREATED BY THE TORNADO'S DESTRUCTIVE WINDS AND ALL THE DEBRIS FLYING THROUGH THE AIR."

Kevin Kloesel, University of Oklahoma meteorologist

THE PHOTO ON THE FACING PAGE WAS TAKEN BY SEVERE WEATHER photographer Jim Reed on April 11, 2002. Jim and his assistant were observing their first tornado of the season—a brown "Liberty Bell"-shaped twister over a bean field outside Pretty Prairie, Kansas. They were accompanied by a Kansas state trooper whose car was parked in front of theirs. Suddenly the tornado made a U-turn and headed directly toward them. Says Reed:

The beautiful tornado spinning at about 80-90 mph had been on the ground for about twenty minutes, crossing our path from left to right. Then it did a U-turn, suddenly changing directions and charging directly at us...

"It had been raining and so it was hard to back up," explained Reed. "The tornado was not picking up debris so it was invisible when it turned toward us." They backed up with difficulty and barely avoided the oncoming twister. In his twenty years as a severe weather photographer, this was Jim Reed's closest call. "I still have nightmares about these storms," he continued, "They're incredible phenomena in every which way on every level."

Texas, the second biggest state in the United States, has vast flatlands where twisters such as this monster can be seen from far away.

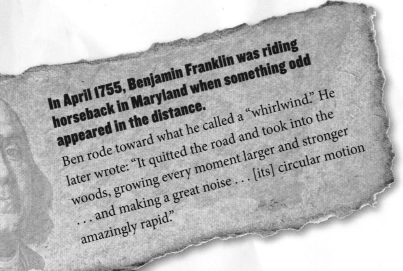

In April 1755, Benjamin Franklin was riding horseback in Maryland when something odd appeared in the distance.

Ben rode toward what he called a "whirlwind." He later wrote: "It quitted the road and took into the woods, growing every moment larger and stronger . . . and making a great noise . . . [its] circular motion amazingly rapid."

Benjamin Franklin made this historic drawing of the dynamics of a waterspout. As for storm chasing, Franklin said, "Some are weather-wise, some are otherwise."

Meteorologists (weather scientists) define a tornado as a fast-spinning column of air that descends from a thunderstorm cloud and touches the Earth's surface. The word tornado comes from *tornare*, which means "to turn" in Latin. Because tornadoes turn and twist as they move, they are also known as twisters.

Tornadoes typically are between one tenth and one quarter of a mile wide—roughly equal to the distance of one or two city blocks and only about one-thousandth the diameter of a hurricane. However, the winds in tornadoes can occasionally top 300 miles per hour (482 km/h)—about 100 miles per hour (161 km/h) faster than the winds in the most powerful hurricanes.

In 2007 meteorologists introduced a new system to rate the strength and estimated wind speeds of tornadoes. Called the Enhanced Fujita Scale (EF), it divides tornadoes into six categories from EF0 to EF5 (see opposite page).

The 2007 Greensburg tornado was an EF5, but fewer than one out of every one hundred tornadoes achieves that status. The winds in most tornadoes whirl at speeds of 110 miles per hour (177 km/h) or less—still plenty strong.

Although the winds inside them are mighty, twisters move forward at an average speed of only about 30 miles per hour (48 km/h). However, they can speed up, slow down, change direction, or stand still. They have even been known to make U-turns and figure 8s. Mountains don't necessarily stop them, as one twister showed by climbing the slope of a 3,300-foot (1,005 m) peak near Blue Ridge, Georgia, and then continuing into the valley beyond. Tornadoes are generally short-lived. A typical twister lasts for less than 15 minutes and travels along the ground for about six miles before fizzling out.

THE FUJITA SCALE

In 2007 meteorologists (weather scientists) introduced the Enhanced Fujita Scale (EF) to rate the strength and estimated wind speeds of tornadoes. Based on a system devised by tornado expert Tetsuya "Ted" Fujita, the EF Scale divides twisters into six categories.

While working at the University of Chicago in the 1970s, Ted Fujita created a machine to help him study tornadoes.

EF Number	Estimated Wind Speed	Typical Damage
EF0	**65-85** mph (105-137 km/h)	Light damage to roofs and tree limbs
EF1	**86-110** mph (138-177 km/h)	Moderate damage, including broken windows and overturned mobile homes
EF2	**111-135** mph (179-217 km/h)	Considerable damage, including big trees uprooted and cars lifted into the air
EF3	**136-165** mph (219-266 km/h)	Severe damage to houses and large buildings
EF4	**166-200** mph (267-322 km/h)	Devastating damage, including the destruction of homes
EF5	**More than 200** mph (322 km/h)	Total or near-total destruction, including the leveling of entire neighborhoods and towns

Tornadoes are born when cold, dry air moving from one direction meets warm, moist air moving in from another direction. Because cold air is heavier, it pushes beneath the warm air. The warm air is forced to rise quickly. Thunderstorms created by this air ballet may begin to rotate, or spin, in places. These rotating regions in thunderstorms sometimes produce tornadoes, but the exact process is not yet fully understood.

The strongest tornadoes often develop in especially intense, rotating thunderstorms called supercells. Besides twisters, supercells produce hail and heavy rainfall. For example, Megan Gardiner recalled that "the hail was probably golf ball size or a little larger" prior to the Greensburg tornado.

The conditions that create a tornado can generate more than one twister. A group of twisters that are produced by a single storm and that share a similar path line are called a tornado family. In 1917 a family of up to eight separate twisters traveled a total of 294 miles (473 km) through Illinois and Indiana. As one tornado died out, another formed to take its place.

Now and then a single twister may develop more than one funnel. Tornadoes with more than one area of rotation inside them are called "multiple vortex" tornadoes. At one point a tornado that struck Wichita Falls, Texas, in 1979 consisted of three separate funnels joined together.

Occasionally when thunderstorms develop over a huge area, dozens of twisters can appear. This is called a tornado outbreak. The largest such event ever recorded in North America, the "Super Outbreak" of April 3–4, 1974, produced an astonishing 148 tornadoes.

Why HAIL often accompanies TORNADOES

"This has to do with the updraft portion of the thunderstorm. Supercell thunderstorms can produce vertical wind speeds exceeding 100 miles per hour at times. This kind of updraft is necessary for strong tornadoes such as the Greensburg tornado. The updraft winds can also suspend fairly large massed objects. Hail begins as very small ice embryos. Super-cooled water droplets continue to make the ice embryos larger and larger until they weigh so much that the updraft winds can no longer support them and they fall to the ground as hail."

Meteorologist Mike Umscheid

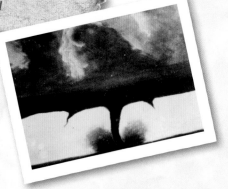

This first photographic image of a tornado was created in 1884.

Tornadoes are spawned when huge masses of warm, moist air collide with large areas of cold, dry air. Add a wind-driven twist and, like a top, a tornado is born.

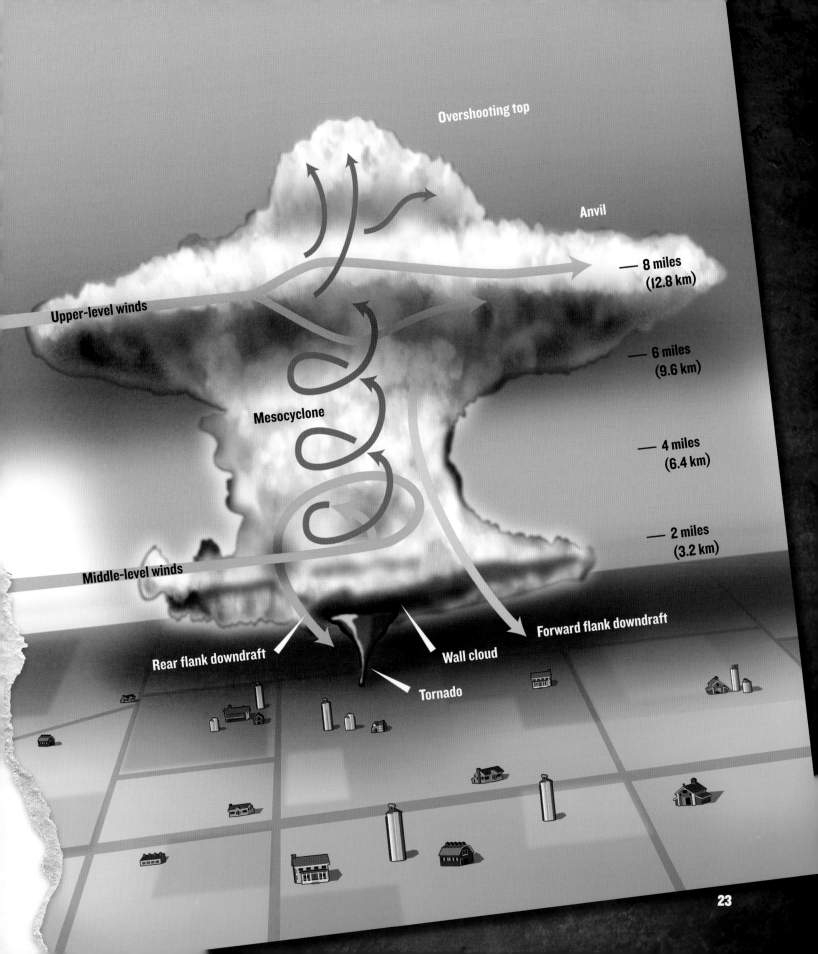

Overshooting top

Anvil

— 8 miles
(12.8 km)

Upper-level winds

— 6 miles
(9.6 km)

Mesocyclone

— 4 miles
(6.4 km)

— 2 miles
(3.2 km)

Middle-level winds

Forward flank downdraft

Rear flank downdraft

Wall cloud

Tornado

Tornadoes in the U.S.A.

Washington

Oregon

Montana

North Dakota

Idaho

South Dakota

Wyoming

Nevada

Nebraska

California

Utah

Colorado

Kansas

Arizona

New Mexico

Oklahoma

PACIFIC
OCEAN

Texas

MEXICO

24

CANADA

L. Superior

Minnesota

Wisconsin

L. Michigan

L. Huron

Michigan

L. Ontario

Maine

Vermont

New Hampshire

New York

Massachusetts

Rhode Island
Connecticut

L. Erie

Pennsylvania

New Jersey

Iowa

Illinois

Indiana

Ohio

Maryland

Delaware

ATLANTIC
OCEAN

Missouri

Kentucky

West
Virginia

Virginia

Washington, D.C.

Tennessee

North Carolina

Arkansas

Mississippi

South
Carolina

Alabama

Georgia

Louisiana

Florida

TORNADOES IN THE U.S.
Selected tornadoes, 1959–2009

F4 or F5 on Fujita scale
winds 207–318 mph

F2 or F5 on Fujita scale
winds 113–206 mph

F0 or F1 on Fujita scale
winds 40–112 mph

NOTE: The tornadoes on this map
represent the pattern of where
tornadoes occur in the United States.
The most powerful tornadoes, with
winds over 200 miles per hour, are
rare, and occur mostly in the plains
and deep south.

Gulf of Mexico

| 0 | 100 | 200 mi |
| 0 | 100 | 200 km |

Tornadoes have often demonstrated their awesome power. A 1979 twister in Vernon, Texas, pulled out 100-foot-tall (30 m) trees by their roots and scattered them like toothpicks across a pasture. A 1999 tornado that demolished an airstrip near Chickasha, Oklahoma, carried a 350-pound (159 kg) airplane wing 70 miles (113 km) before dropping it.

There have been many incredible stories of people being picked up—and sometimes safely set down—by tornadoes. An 1899 twister in Kirksville, Missouri, lifted a boy and a horse into the air. Eyewitnesses later claimed that they saw the horse flying over a church steeple. After flying hundreds of yards, the boy and the horse were dropped down onto the ground. "At one time the horse was directly over me," the boy explained, adding that he had been scared that the animal would kick him. L. Frank Baum's famous novel *The Wonderful Wizard of Oz,* with its memorable tornado scene, was partially inspired by incidents like this.

Unfortunately, people's encounters with tornadoes often end unhappily, for two main reasons. First, tornadoes cause buildings to collapse, crushing and trapping people inside. Second, they turn everyday objects like tree branches, nails, pieces of glass, and roof shingles into deadly missiles.

"As a kid, I was absolutely terrified of storms, but at the same time fascinated. I looked at every book I could get my hands on that had pictures of tornadoes. I watched *The Wizard of Oz* every year just to see the tornado."

Rick Smith, National Weather Service meteorologist and tornado expert

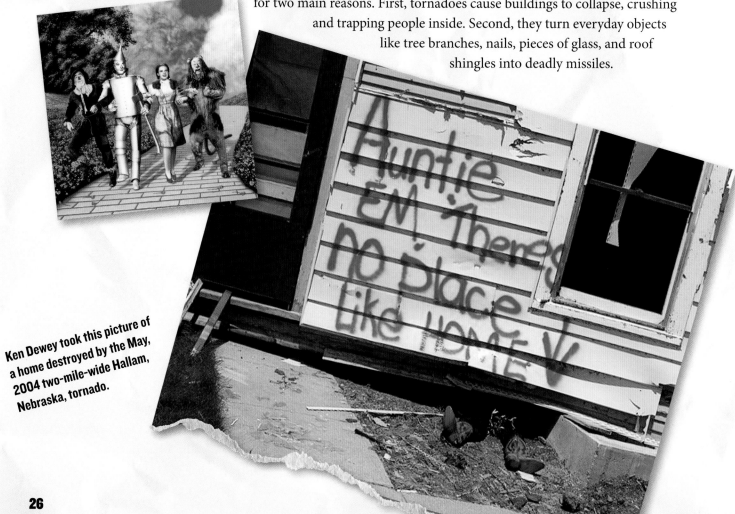

Ken Dewey took this picture of a home destroyed by the May, 2004 two-mile-wide Hallam, Nebraska, tornado.

A fanciful rendition of objects picked up by a tornado and swirling through its funnel

An Inside View...

In June 1928 Kansas farmer Will Keller became one of the few people to look up inside a tornado and live to tell about it. Mr. Keller was about to enter his family's storm shelter when he stopped to glance at the sky.

"The great shaggy end of the funnel hung directly overhead. Everything was as still as death," Keller later reported. "There was a strong gassy odor and it seemed that I could not breathe. There was a screaming hissing sound coming directly from the end of the funnel. I looked up and to my astonishment I saw right up into the heart of the tornado. There was a circular opening in the center of the funnel, about 50 or 100 feet in diameter, and extending straight upward for a distance of at least one half mile. The walls of this opening were of rotating clouds and the whole was made brilliantly visible by constant flashes of lightning which zigzagged from side to side."

The 1999 Oklahoma City tornado generated winds of 318 mph (512 km/h), the strongest winds ever recorded on Earth.

Tornado Talk

Supercell

Especially intense, rotating thunderstorms where the strongest tornadoes often form

Funnel Cloud

A whirling cloud that becomes a tornado if it touches the ground

Tornado

Fast-spinning column of air that touches our planet's surface

Tornado Family

A group of tornadoes that are produced by a single storm and that follow a similar path

Waterspout

Twister that travels over the ocean or a lake and sucks water into its swirling winds

Tornado Outbreak

The occurrence of a large number of tornadoes in a region over a period of hours. This satellite image shows the storms that produced the deadly outbreak of 87 tornadoes crossing the midwestern and southern United States on May 5-6, 2008.

KILLER TORNADOES

True Stories of Deadly Twisters

Meteorologist Daphne Zaras took this photo
of the 1999 storm that spawned the Chickasha,
Oklahoma, tornado.

The Tri-State Tornado

ABOUT 12:55 P.M. ON MARCH 18, 1925, A TWISTER TOUCHED DOWN near Ellington, Missouri. It was so large that many witnesses said they saw only "a blackness" coming their way. Those who got a clear view of this monster of monsters reported that at times it was composed of two or even three separate funnels.

After ripping apart homes and yanking out trees in southeastern Missouri, the twister moved into Illinois, where it displayed another remarkable quality. Instead of fizzling out, it kept going, gouging out a nearly mile-wide path of destruction. A girl explained what happened to her school in Gorham, Illinois:

We were in a classroom and it suddenly got so dark we couldn't see. All the children rushed to the windows. Teacher made us go back to our seats. All we could see at the windows was that it was black—like night almost. Then the wind struck the school. The walls seemed to fall in all around us.

Heading on a northeasterly path, the tornado destroyed much of Murphysboro, Illinois, killing 234 people in that town. At West Frankfort, Illinois, miners in an underground coal mine heard a roar as the tornado struck the earth above them. The twister sent a blast of air down a mine shaft, collapsing timbers and extinguishing the lights. Using their hat lamps to illuminate the way, all 800 men climbed out of the mine safely.

HERALD CH

14th YEAR
No. 289   Registered U. S. Patent Office
Copyright, 1925, News and Examiner

Telephone Main 5000

FRIDAY, M

848 DEAD, 2,90

In the Twinkling of an Eye

The Tri-State tornado claimed 695 lives, the most lives of any tornado in history. Some experts believe that if a similar tornado occurred today, no more than 50 or 60 lives would be lost. This is because our 21st-century warning systems allow people to take shelter well before a twister strikes.

EXAMINER

1 20, 1925.   M*   TWO PARTS   PRICE 3 CENT

HURT LATEST TOLL OF TORNADO

Murphysboro Was No More

After crossing Illinois, the tornado entered southern Indiana. It completely demolished the town of Griffin before ending its 219-mile (353 km) journey. Because it traveled through three states—Missouri, Illinois, and Indiana—this memorable storm was named the Tri-State tornado.

Super Outbreak, 1974

In early April of 1974 thunderstorms and supercells formed over a huge region of the United States, spawning a gigantic outbreak of 148 tornadoes. The barrage began on April 3 when a farmer near Morris, Illinois, saw a relatively weak tornado kick up some dirt in a field.

Over the next 18 hours, tornadoes touched down in 13 states and part of Canada. The Xenia, Ohio, tornado was the deadliest of the twisters. Its 300 mph (483 km/h) winds destroyed half of Xenia, causing 35 deaths. This tornado was so powerful that it lifted a tractor-trailer skyward and dropped it onto the roof of a bowling alley. Documents swept out of homes in Xenia were later found 200 miles (322 km) away.

An announcer/helicopter pilot for a Louisville radio station alerted many people in Kentucky. On the afternoon of April 3, Dick Gilbert was several hundred feet up in his chopper when he noticed something unusual in the sky. He told his listeners:

Low clouds—very black, low clouds. And it is swirling around, and it looks like smoke underneath it. Yes! There's one starting, yes, dipping down from the bottom of the cloud. The power transformers have been blowing regularly in the path of this thing—big, large explosions of blue and white light.

By describing the tornado's path, Gilbert enabled his listeners to seek a place of safety. Thanks partly to Dick Gilbert, many lives were spared.

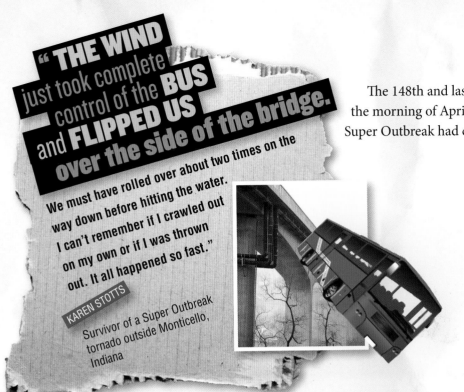

"THE WIND just took complete control of the BUS and FLIPPED US over the side of the bridge.

We must have rolled over about two times on the way down before hitting the water. I can't remember if I crawled out on my own or if I was thrown out. It all happened so fast."

KAREN STOTTS
Survivor of a Super Outbreak tornado outside Monticello, Indiana

The 148th and last twister of the Super Outbreak struck on the morning of April 4 in North Carolina. By then, the Super Outbreak had claimed 335 lives and injured 6,000 others.

"IT WAS VERY HARD TO BREATHE AND I FELT THAT I WAS ABOUT TO SUFFOCATE ... BY THE TIME DADDY TOOK US INTO THE CLOSET I WAS CRYING AND YELLING AND SCREAMING. THEN WHEN I HEARD THIS LOUD NOISE LIKE A TRAIN HITTING OUR HOUSE, I THOUGHT WE WERE GOING TO DIE."

Allison Hall, describing the Wichita Falls tornado

Wichita Falls, Texas
Tornado of 1979

At 5:50 P.M. on April 10, 1979, the emergency sirens were sounded in Wichita Falls, a city of 120,000 people in northern Texas. "Take cover immediately," TV viewers were warned. Then their sets went black as a giant tornado knocked out the city's electricity.

A powerful, violent twister scatters debris over Pampa, Texas, on June 8, 1995. This tornado was similar to the one that struck Wichita Falls in 1979.

Dennis Spruill sought shelter in his bathroom, where he grabbed onto the toilet. "I could feel the tornado pulling my hair and my clothes upward," he later recalled. "I could feel it tugging on me as I held on for dear life."

Some Wichita Falls residents tried to flee by automobile. That was a bad choice, for a car is a dangerous place to be in a twister, especially one with winds approaching 300 miles per hour (483 km/h). Of the 46 fatalities in Wichita Falls, 25 were vehicle-related.

In 2008, one of the biggest tornado outbreaks in U.S. history occurred at an unusual time of year for twisters. Starting on the afternoon of February 5 and continuing until the next morning, a series of supercell thunderstorms rolled across much of the United States.

THE SUPERCELLS PRODUCED AT LEAST **92** TORNADOES THAT STRUCK **10** STATES.

One tornado destroyed about 20 buildings on the Union University campus in Jackson, Tennessee. A number of students were trapped in the debris. Although all of them were rescued, more than 50 injured students had to be hospitalized. Aaron Gilbert, who was injured slightly by flying glass, said that after the tornado, Union University "looked like a war zone."

The February 5-6 outbreak, which claimed 59 lives, ushered in a devastating year of tornadoes. By late August of 2008, about 2,000 tornadoes had been counted in the United States—twice as many as usually occur in an entire year.

June 10, 2008: A spinning supercell dropped a tornado from the sky. It tore up a few farm fields outside Orchard, Iowa, then lifted before damaging the silos and building in the photo. Note the flag being pulled *toward* the twister.

"TO ME IT sounded like if you stand behind A JET ENGINE ...

Then the windows broke and I could feel glass flying through the air. The lights were flickering. I could hear the walls crunch, and debris was flying. It was like being on the inside of a tin can and it's crushing in on you."

AARON GILBERT

recounting his experience in the tornado that hit Union University

The shaggy funnel of a strong tornado churns up red mud as it crosses the Palo Duro Canyon in west Texas on March 28, 2007.

Longest distance on the ground	219 miles (352 km)	1925 Tri-State Tornado
Most time on the ground	three and a half hours	1925 Tri-State Tornado
Greatest forward speed by a major tornado	73 mph (117 km/h)	1925 Tri-State Tornado
Widest known tornado	2 miles (3.2 km)	2004 Hallam, Nebraska
Highest wind speeds ever recorded on the planet	318 mph (512 km/h)	Oklahoma City Tornado of 1999
Largest tornado outbreak in North America	148 tornadoes	"Super Outbreak" of April 3-4, 1974
Most likely month for tornadoes	May	June is the second and April is the third
Nation most often struck by tornadoes	United States	about 1,000 of the world's twisters per year
Oldest tornado records	as much as 1,000 years old	from China
Most people killed by a tornado	as many as 1,300	in the Asian country of Bangladesh on April 26, 1989

Five DEADLIEST U.S. Tornadoes

Deaths	Date	Place
1 695	March 18, 1925	**Tri-State Tornado** (Missouri, Illinois, Indiana)
2 317	May 7, 1840	**Natchez Tornado** (Mississippi)
3 255	May 27, 1896	**St. Louis Tornado** (Missouri)
4 216	April 5, 1936	**Tupelo Tornado** (Mississippi)
5 203	April 6, 1936	**Gainesville Tornado** (Georgia)

TWISTER PREDICTION

How We Know They're Coming

A storm chaser plants a weather probe in the path of a South Dakota tornado.

"TORNADOES ARE ONE OF THE MOST DIFFICULT WEATHER HAZARDS TO FORECAST ACCURATELY. WE KNOW SOME OF THE INGREDIENTS FOR MAKING A TORNADO—LIKE WARM, MOIST AIR AND WIND SHEAR—BUT WE DON'T KNOW THEM ALL."

Meteorologist Kevin Kloesel

ON MARCH 20, 1948, A TORNADO STRUCK TINKER AIR FORCE BASE near Oklahoma City, Oklahoma, injuring eight people and extensively damaging aircraft and buildings. Two weather forecasters, Major Ernest Fawbush and Captain Robert Miller, were given the job of predicting when future tornadoes might strike the base. On March 25, Fawbush and Miller saw that conditions were similar to those that had produced the tornado just five days earlier. They warned that another twister could strike.

The chances of two twisters five days apart hitting the same locale were about one in 20 million. Yet that's what the weather charts indicated. Fawbush and Miller stuck to their forecast. Airplanes were parked in hangars to protect them. Incoming air traffic was sent to other fields. People on the base sought places of safety.

Early that evening, a second twister struck Tinker Air Force Base, just as the two forecasters had predicted. Thanks to their warning, no one was killed or injured, and damage to aircraft was minimized. Fawbush and Miller's warning on that spring day in 1948 marked the birth of modern tornado forecasting.

Their accurate warning also helped change weather forecasters' attitudes about making tornado predictions. Previously, it had been thought that forecasting tornadoes was impossible. Fawbush and Miller proved not only that tornadoes can sometimes be predicted but also that issuing warnings about them can save lives.

Inside the Tornado

This sequence of photos was captured by a weather probe like the one shown on page 46. The images show a South Dakota tornado approaching the camera, passing directly over the camera, then receding in the distance.

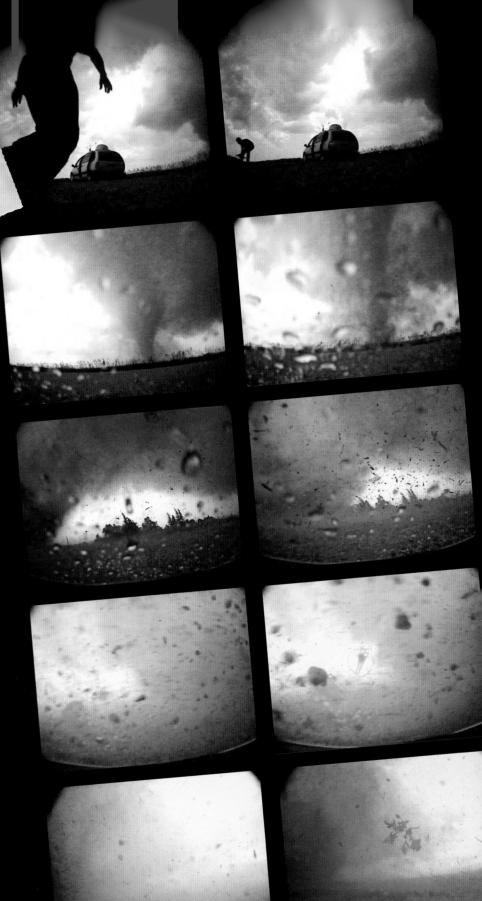

The large red spot at the center of this Doppler radar image shows the violent tornado bearing down on Greensburg, Kansas.

Using a radar system called "Doppler on Wheels," or DOW, a team of research scientists measured the wind speed of the powerful Oklahoma City tornado at 318 mph (512 km/h). This is the highest wind speed ever recorded on our planet.

Since then, scientists have developed new tools that help tornado forecasters. Weather satellites are a key tool. Although they do not spot individual tornadoes, they identify supercells and other thunderstorms that might produce twisters. Satellites also enable meteorologists to track the movements of these storms.

Radar has been used in weather forecasting since the 1940s. Radar can detect raindrops and hail—phenomena associated with thunderstorms—by bouncing signals off them. During the 1980s and 1990s, a new kind of radar was installed at U.S. weather stations. Called Doppler radar for the 19th-century Austrian physicist Christian Doppler, it can detect and measure air motion within a storm, providing clues about where to look for tornadoes. If the tornado is close to Doppler radar, the radar can even identify an actual tornado.

"Meteorologists rely heavily on Doppler radar to study severe local storms such as the one that struck Greensburg," says Mike Umscheid. Because of the Greensburg tornado's enormous size, he could actually see the vortex moving on his radar screen. Usually, though, it is difficult to find tornadoes by using radar unless the twister is nearby. Often the clearest evidence of a tornado revealed by Doppler radar is a hook echo visible on the radar screen. "It is called a hook echo because it is a radar image that takes on the shape of a fishhook," Umscheid explains. A hook echo indicates rotating motion in the storm that may result in tornadoes.

Because even Doppler radar generally doesn't provide conclusive evidence of a tornado, there is another component to our nation's tornado warning

Storm-chasing professor Ken Dewey's portable radar device allows him to track potential tornado-producing weather.

program. "We get reports from trained storm spotters," says Mike Umscheid. About 300,000 volunteer "severe weather spotters" help the 122 local National Weather Service forecast offices. Severe weather spotters come from many walks of life and have been trained to observe and report tornadoes. A hook echo on a meteorologist's radar screen combined with a trained spotter's report of a twister on the ground is conclusive evidence that a tornado is in an area.

Tornado Watches and Warnings

The Storm Prediction Center, a special National Weather Service office in Norman, Oklahoma, issues tornado watches. A typical tornado watch is issued for a vast region covering about 25,000 square miles (64,750 sq km). A tornado watch doesn't mean that twisters have been seen in an area but that weather conditions are ripe for tornado formation. People in a region for which a tornado watch has been issued should keep track of weather bulletins on TV or radio to see if a tornado warning will be issued.

Tornado warnings are extremely serious. "A tornado warning means that a tornado has been spotted on the ground or that the Doppler weather radar shows that the storm is rotating fast enough to produce a tornado," says meteorologist Daphne Thompson.

TORNADO WARNING

DO

DO TAKE COVER IMMEDIATELY
If you have a basement or storm cellar, go there. If not, hide in an interior bathroom or closet on the lowest floor. You want to put as many walls between you and the tornado as possible.

DO PROTECT YOUR HEAD
Protecting your head is the most important thing you can do. Put on a bicycle helmet during tornado warnings.

DON'T

DON'T TAKE SHELTER IN YOUR CAR
If you're in a car when a tornado approaches, get out and find shelter. If none is available, lie down low in a ditch or depression. Don't seek shelter under highway overpasses, for tornado winds can become even faster in these spaces.

This photo of a 2008 Kansas twister illustrates how tornadoes take on the color of the debris they churn up.

SEVERE WEATHER
RESEARCH UNIT #2

EXPLORER

KANSAS
559 ATU

SKYWARN

The Twister Sisters

Every spring two scientists from Minnesota, Peggy Willenberg and Melanie Metz, drive through Tornado Alley to places where forecasters say twisters are likely to develop in order to view and photograph them. In an average year the two friends, who call themselves the Twister Sisters, see about 10 tornadoes up close. Willenberg recalls the first tornado she saw with her Twister Sister:

"After a long day of driving to Nebraska, we watched a severe thunderstorm become organized into a supercell. The process was very methodical and time consuming.

It was as if a meteorology textbook were laid out there in the prairie and we could take our time reading it. The tornado was a perfect white cone, and it moved majestically over the barren landscape. Suddenly it disappeared. But we had the privilege to watch its entire evolution."

Scientists still have many questions about tornadoes and how they form. Sometimes they answer them by "storm chasing"— approaching twisters to study them. This sounds dangerous, but the scientists have equipment that helps them safely track the twisters' location and movement.

"In 1994 and 1995, tornado scientists from around the country used the most advanced weather instruments to try and figure out how tornadoes form," explains Dr. Kloesel. "The project was called VORTEX. Although we learned about some of the ingredients that combine to make a tornado, we still don't have the exact recipe for how a tornado is created.

"Since 1995, we have been working on new weather instruments to try and see inside a tornado. In 2009, scientists tried out these new instruments. We used radars that enabled us to see much more detail within the storms. Remote-controlled aircraft measured weather conditions in and around thunderstorms and tornadoes. This project, VORTEX-2, is the most extensive study of tornadoes ever attempted."

Added Daphne Thompson: "As part of VORTEX-2, mobile radar trucks got incredibly close to tornadoes to gather data. Weather balloons were launched into and around storms to measure their wind speed and direction, temperature, and pressure. Teams of photographers videotaped clouds that created the storms along with the tornadoes that formed. And small packages of instruments that measured temperature and humidity were placed within the path of tornadoes."

On June 5, 2009, a tornado headed directly toward a VORTEX-2 team in Goshen County, Wyoming. It remained on the ground for 25 minutes, allowing itself to be thoroughly filmed and measured before the unexpected occurred. Amazingly, the tornado tilted so the team could see inside it from the top! Within its vortex spiraled a slender second twister.

The VORTEX-2 project ran for six weeks during the summers of both 2009 and 2010. The $10.5 million project employed more than 100 scientists and used 40 mobile vehicles to study numerous supercells. The information gathered by the project will allow scientists to predict more precisely when and where tornadoes form. They will then be able to warn the rest of us more quickly and more accurately.

"**M**ETEOROLOGISTS ARE DETECTIVES. WE SEARCH FOR CLUES IN AN ATTEMPT TO SOLVE THE MYSTERY OF HOW A TORNADO FORMS. FOR EXAMPLE, WE USE VIDEO CAMERAS—WE CAN SLOW THE VIDEO MOTION DOWN AND STUDY THE DETAILS JUST LIKE A SLOW MOTION REPLAY DURING A SPORTING EVENT."

Meteorologist Kevin Kloesel

Two graduate students set up a pod that measures air pressure and temperature within a tornado. It also supports a camera and a GPS system. This pod was designed for the VORTEX-2 project.

Tornado Scrapbook

Meteorology students observe and study a 2004 Kansas supercell.

A 2010 twister that started as a water-spout scatters debris as it rips through Lennox Head, a coastal Australian town.

Hurricanes frequently spin off tornadoes. In 2005 Hurricane Wilma spawned 10 tornadoes in Florida.

This Arkansas storm shelter saved a family of four whose home was destroyed by a 2008 tornado. It was built by the homeowner's grandfather in 1925 and had been used twice before.

Powerful winds knocked down trees, ripped off roofs, and shattered windows as a 2008 EF2 tornado tore through downtown Atlanta, Georgia.

A tornado spins through downtown Miami, twisting and turning through the city. Despite how scary it looks, this tornado only injured 5 people.

Where Tornadoes Occur Around the World

NORTH AMERICA

PACIFIC OCEAN

ATLANTIC OCEAN

SOUTH AMERICA

TORNADO THREAT

High

Low

ARCTIC OCEAN

EUROPE

ASIA

PACIFIC
OCEAN

AFRICA

INDIAN
OCEAN

AUSTRALIA

ANTARCTICA

GLOSSARY

Air pressure (or atmospheric pressure): the force that air exerts on an area

Anvil: the shape of the top of a thunderstorm cloud caused by winds blowing the top of the cloud downstream

Doppler radar: radar that has the ability to detect and measure motion, including rotating winds within a thunderstorm that may produce tornadoes

Downdraft: a downward moving current of air

Funnel (or funnel cloud): a whirling cloud that becomes a tornado if it touches the ground; a tornado is often referred to as a funnel

Hail: lumps or pellets of ice that fall from the sky; hail often accompanies tornadoes but also often occurs without a tornado appearing

Hook echo: the portion of a thunderstorm on a radar image that takes the shape of a fishhook; a hook echo indicates rotating motion in a storm that sometimes results in tornadoes

Mesocyclone: a spinning updraft in a supercell thunderstorm that exists prior to the formation of a tornado

Meteorologist: a weather scientist

Prediction: a statement that something is likely to occur in the future

Radar: an instrument that can detect and locate objects by bouncing signals off them

Roping out: a process in which some tornadoes take on a rope-like appearance toward the end of their existence

Severe weather spotters: volunteers who have been trained to observe and report tornadoes

Supercell: especially intense, rotating thunderstorms where the strongest tornadoes often form

Tornado: a fast-spinning column of air that touches our planet's surface

Tornado Alley: a wide north-south area roughly in the middle of the U.S. where many tornadoes strike

Tornado family: a group of tornadoes that are produced by a single storm and that share a similar path

Tornado outbreak: the occurrence of a large number of tornadoes in a region over a period of hours

Tornado warning: message informing people that an actual tornado has been detected or is extremely likely in an area

Tornado watch: message informing people that conditions in a region are ripe for thunderstorms that produce tornadoes

Twister: another name for a tornado

Vortex (plural vortices or vortexes): the tube-shaped main portion of a tornado

Waterspout: twister that travels over the ocean or a lake and sucks water into its swirling winds

Weather forecaster: person trained to predict future weather conditions

Weather satellites: spacecraft that monitor the Earth's weather

SOME WEBSITES TO EXPLORE

For lots of interesting tornado information and pictures:
http://kids.nationalgeographic.com/kids/photos/tornadoes/

Basic tornado information for kids:
http://www.weatherwizkids.com/weather-tornado.htm

For facts about tornadoes and tornado safety advice:
http://www.nssl.noaa.gov/edu/safety/tornadoguide.html

For the scientifically-minded, this site answers just about any question you might have about tornadoes:
http://www.spc.noaa.gov/faq/tornado/

For an overview of the VORTEX projects with many links to pictures:
http://www.vortex2.org/home/

To see inside a tornado: http://www.huffingtonpost.com/2009/06/08/rare-look-inside-a-tornad_n_212538.html

BIBLIOGRAPHY

Blown Away: The May 4, 2007 Tornado—The Path of Destruction and Road to Recovery of Greensburg, Kansas. Greensburg, Kansas: The Kiowa County Signal, 2008.

Bradford, Marlene. *Scanning the Skies: A History of Tornado Forecasting.* Norman: University of Oklahoma Press, 2001.

Church, C., D. Burgess, C. Doswell, and R. Davies-Jones, editors. *The Tornado: Its Structure, Dynamics, Prediction, and Hazards.* Washington, DC: American Geophysical Union, 1993.

Felknor, Peter S. *The Tri-State Tornado: The Story of America's Greatest Tornado Disaster.* Ames: Iowa State University Press, 1992.

Grazulis, Thomas P. *The Tornado: Nature's Ultimate Windstorm.* Norman: University of Oklahoma Press, 2001.

Levine, Mark. *F5: Devastation, Survival, and the Most Violent Tornado Outbreak of the Twentieth Century.* New York: Hyperion, 2007.

Rosenfeld, Jeffrey. *Eye of the Storm: Inside the World's Deadliest Hurricanes, Tornadoes, and Blizzards.* New York: Plenum, 1999.

Svenvold, Mark. *Big Weather: Chasing Tornadoes in the Heart of America.* New York: Holt, 2005.

FOR YOUNG READERS

Berger, Melvin and Gilda Berger. *Do Tornadoes Really Twist?: Questions and Answers About Tornadoes and Hurricanes.* New York: Scholastic Reference, 2000.

Claybourne, Anna. *Tornadoes.* Brookfield, Connecticut: Copper Beech Books, 2000.

Grace, Catherine O'Neill. *Forces of Nature: The Awesome Power of Volcanoes, Earthquakes, and Tornadoes.* Washington, DC: National Geographic Society, 2004.

Jeffrey, Gary. *Tornadoes & Superstorms.* New York: Rosen, 2007.

Mogil, H. Michael. *Tornadoes.* Stillwater, Minnesota: Voyageur Press, 2001.

Nicolson, Cynthia Pratt. *Tornado!* Tonawanda, New York: Kids Can Press, 2003.

Simon, Seymour. *Tornadoes.* New York: Morrow Junior Books, 1999.

SURVIVORS & WITNESSES
Interviews by the Authors

Greensburg, Kansas
Mark Anderson, Dea Corns, Megan Gardiner,
Janice Haney, Sheri Taylor

Jackson, Tennessee
Aaron Gilbert

Tornado Alley
Dick McGowan
The Twister Sisters, Melanie Metz
and Peggy Willenberg

Wichita Falls, Texas
Allison, Emogene, and William Hall
Dennis Spruill

TORNADO SCIENTISTS

Dr. Harold Brooks
*Research Meteorologist and Head,
Mesoscale Applications Group at NOAA's
National Severe Storms Laboratory*

Professor Ken Dewey
*Regional Climatologist, High Plains
Regional Climate Center,
University of Nebraska*

Dr. Kevin A. Kloesel
*Associate Dean for Public Service and Outreach,
College of Atmospheric and Geographic Sciences,
University of Oklahoma*

Rick Smith
*Warning Coordination Meteorologist,
National Weather Service-Norman Forecast Office,
Norman, Oklahoma*

Daphne Thompson
*Meteorologist/Educational Outreach Coordinator,
Cooperative Institute for Mesoscale Meteorological
Studies, NOAA's National Severe Storms Laboratory*

Mike Umscheid
*National Weather Service Forecast
Meteorologist, Dodge City, Kansas*

Message from Megan Gardiner, whose quotes come from a narrative she wrote in 2008 about her Greensburg Tornado experience:

I'm 18 years old and just graduated from Greensburg High School. I love volleyball, also basketball, and I did track for a few years, plus I participated in band. I'm a pretty good student, so I was in the National Honor Society and sophomore year I was elected vice president of my class. For the past 3-4 years I have been a lifeguard and really enjoyed doing that. I'm also active in my church.

My parents encouraged me to write about my tornado experience. That way I could get my feelings out and on paper so I wouldn't have to hold them in. It was easy for me to write because that experience played in my head 24/7, nonstop. I am happy I wrote it because if I have kids they will be able to read what my family went through.

Message from our consultant, Dr. Kevin A. Kloesel, who works in the National Weather Center building in Norman, Oklahoma, with more than 500 scientists who are doing research on severe weather:

Every year I visit schools and talk to thousands of children about weather and weather safety. I also teach meteorology classes at the University of Oklahoma, where the weather researchers and forecasters of the future are learning more about all types of severe weather, and how to make you safe when severe weather hits.

My interest in weather started with Little League baseball. The rain delays led me to want to learn more about weather. I still love to attend baseball games, and as a hobby I study how weather affects performance in sports.

Published by National Geographic Partners, LLC. All rights reserved. Reproduction of the whole or any part of the contents without written permission from the publisher is prohibited.

STAFF FOR THIS BOOK

Priyanka Lamichhane,
Project Editor

Lori Epstein,
Illustrations Editor

David M. Seager,
Art Director

Grace Hill,
Associate Managing Editor

Lewis R. Bassford,
Production Manager

Kate Olesin,
Editorial Assistant

Susan Borke,
Legal and Business Affairs

MANUFACTURING AND QUALITY MANAGEMENT

Christopher A. Liedel,
Chief Financial Officer

Phillip L. Schlosser,
Senior Vice President

Chris Brown,
Technical Director

Nicole Elliott,
Manager

Rachel Faulise,
Manager

Robert L. Barr,
Manager

ILLUSTRATION CREDITS

Cover, Alan R Moller/ Stone/ Getty Images; Back cover, Jim Reed; All photocomposite illustrations by David M. Seager

2-3, Reed Timmer and Dean Schoeneck/ Jim Reed Photography/ Corbis; 4 (bottom), Claudia Carlsen/ Shutterstock; 4 (top), Courtesy of the Ohio Historical Society; 4 (center), Jonathan Blair/ Corbis; 6-7, Mike Scantlin; 8, Shutterstock; 9 (inset), Dan Gillig; 9, Elaine Ray, 10, Mike Theiss/ NationalGeographicStock.com; 11 (top), Elaine Ray; 11 (bottom), Green Bear/ Shutterstock; 12-13, Greg Henshall/ FEMA ; 14-15, Jeremy Lock/ National Geographic My Shot/ NationalGeographicStock.com; 16-17, Jim Reed; 18-19, Chuck Doswell/ Visuals Unlimited/ Corbis; 20 (top), iStockphoto.com; 20 (bottom), NOAA; 21 (top center), University of Chicago Department of Public Relations; 21 (A), Jonathan Lenz/ Shutterstock; 21 (B), David Koscheck/ Shutterstock; 21 (C), Dianne Maire/ Shutterstock; 21 (D), Laura Clay-Ballard/ iStockphoto.com; 21 (E), jam4travel/ Shutterstock; 21 (F), jam4travel/ Shutterstock; 22 (top), HABRDA/ Shutterstock; 22 (bottom), NOAA; 23, Illustration by Joe LeMonnier; 26 (left), MGM/ The Kobal Collection/ The Picture Desk; 26 (right), Ken Dewey; 27 (top), pzAxe/ Shutterstock; 27 (top left), Tyler Olson/ Shutterstock; 27 (top right), Soundsnaps/ Shutterstock; 27 (bottom), Yuri Arcurs/ Shutterstock; 28-29, OAR/ ERL/ National Severe Storms Laboratory/ NOAA; 30 (bottom right), Jim Reed/ Jim Reed Photography - Severe &/ Corbis; 30 (bottom left), Jim Nelson/ Shutterstock; 30 (top), Carsten Peter/ NationalGeographicStock.com; 31 (top), Photo by Greg Eliason, from "Forces of Nature," courtesy of National Geographic/Graphic Films; 31 (bottom left), Christina Heliker/ USGS; 31 (bottom right), NOAA; 32-33, Daphne Zaras/ NOAA; 34-35, University of Illinois at Urbana-Champaign; 36 (left), Claudine Bosseler/ Shutterstock; 36 (right), Margo Harrison/ Shutterstock; 37, Fred Smith; 38, Alan R Moller/ Stone/ Getty Images; 39 (bottom), Bearman/ Shutterstock; 39 (top left), Amy Johansson/ Shutterstock; 39 (top right), leodor/ Shutterstock; 40 (bottom), Gualtiero Boffi/ Shutterstock; 40 (top), Sebastian Crocker/ Shutterstock; 41, Lori Mehmen/ Associated Press; 42-43, Gene Rhoden/ Weatherpix Stock Images; 46-47, Carsten Peter/ NationalGeographicStock.com; 48-49, Timothy Samaras; 50, Jim Reed; 50 (top), Dodge City Warning Center/ NOAA; 51, Ken Dewey; 53, Jim Reed; 54, Peggy Willenberg & Melanie Metz; 54, Keith Webber Jr./ iStockphoto.com; 54, Peggy Willenberg & Melanie Metz; 54, Peggy Willenberg & Melanie Metz; 55, Steve Sisney/ Daily Oklahoman/ Associated Press; 56-57, Miami Herald/ Getty Images; 56 (top left), Jim Reed/ Corbis; 56 (bottom), NOAA; 56 (top right), Ross Tuckerman/ AFP/ Getty Images; 57 (left), Dave Martin/ Associated Press; 57 (right), Charles S. Powell/ FEMA ; 60, INGAJA/ Shutterstock; 61, Kate Bibisheva/ Shutterstock

LIBRARY OF CONGRESS CATALOGING-IN-PUBLICATION DATA

Fradin, Judith Bloom, author.
Tornado!: the story behind these twisting, turning, spinning, and spiraling storms / By Judith Bloom Fradin and Dennis Brindell Fradin.
    p. cm.
Includes bibliographical references and index.
ISBN 978-1-4263-0779-9 (hardcover: alk. paper)—
ISBN 978-1-4263-0780-5 (library binding: alk. paper)
    1. Tornadoes. I. Fradin, Dennis B. (Dennis Brindell), 1945-, author. II. Title.
QC955.F77 2011
551.55'3—dc22
                                    2010042813

Since 1888, the National Geographic Society has funded more than 12,000 research, exploration, and preservation projects around the world. The Society receives funds from National Geographic Partners, LLC, funded in part by your purchase. A portion of the proceeds from this book supports this vital work. To learn more, visit natgeo.com/info.

NATIONAL GEOGRAPHIC and Yellow Border Design are trademarks of the National Geographic Society, used under license.

For more information, please visit nationalgeographic.com, call 1-877-873-6846, or write to the following address:

National Geographic Partners
1145 17th Street N.W.,
Washington, D.C. 20036-4688 U.S.A.

Visit us online at
www.nationalgeographic.com/books
Librarians visit us at
ngchildrensbooks.com

For information about special discounts for bulk purchases, please contact National Geographic Books Special Sales: specialsales@natgeo.com

For rights or permissions inquiries, please contact National Geographic Books Subsidiary Rights: bookrights@natgeo.com

Printed in Hong Kong
21/PPHK/8